THE
gluten, wheat and dairy free
COOKBOOK

NICOLA GRAIMES

𝑝

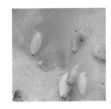

This is a Parragon Book
First published in 2004

Parragon
Queen Street House
4 Queen Street
Bath
BA1 1HE
UK

Designed and produced by
THE BRIDGEWATER BOOK COMPANY

Nutritional Facts and Analyses: *Charlotte Watts*
Photography: *Clive Bozzard-Hill*
Home Economist: *Philippa Vanstone*
Stylist: *Angela Macfarlane*

The publishers would like to thank the following companies for the loan
of props: *Dartington Crystal, Marlux Mills, Maxwell & Williams, Lifestyle Collections,
Viners & Oneida and John Lewis.*

Printed in China

ISBN: 1-40543-885-1

NOTES FOR THE READER

This book uses metric and imperial measurements. Follow the same units of measurement throughout; do not mix metric and imperial. All spoon measurements are level, unless otherwise stated: teaspoons are assumed to be 5 ml and tablespoons are assumed to be 15 ml.

Individual vegetables such as potatoes are medium and pepper is freshly ground black pepper.

Some of the recipes require stock. If you use commercially made stock granules or cubes, these can have a relatively high salt content, so do not add any further salt. If you make your own stock, keep the fat and salt content to a minimum. Don't fry the vegetables before simmering – just simmer the vegetables, herbs and meat, poultry or fish in water and strain. Meat and poultry stocks should be strained, cooled and refrigerated before use so that the fat from the meat rises to the top and solidifies – it can then be easily removed and this reduces the saturated fat content of the meal. Homemade stocks should be stored in the refrigerator and used within two days, or frozen in usable portions and labelled.

Cooking times may vary as a result of the type of oven used. Ovens should be preheated to the specified temperature. If using a fan-assisted oven, check the manufacturer's instructions for adjusting the time and temperature.

The values of the nutritional analysis for each recipe refer to a single serving, or a single slice where relevant. The calorific value given is in KCal (Kilocalories). The carbohydrate figure includes starches and sugars, with the sugar value then given separately. The fat figure is likewise, the total fat, with the saturated part then given separately.

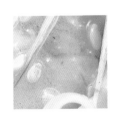

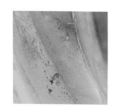

contents

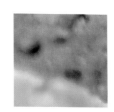

Introduction

A Fresh Start

One in six people in the UK are said to suffer from some form of allergy, and two of the most common food groups that may cause an adverse reaction are grains and dairy products. A gluten-, wheat- and dairy-free diet was once regarded as nutrient-deficient, restrictive and difficult to follow, but it is now much easier to adopt, thanks to a growing acceptance and understanding of these dietary problems by the medical profession, along with the wide availability of so many alternative ingredients. If you have a food allergy or intolerance, it need not spoil your pleasure in cooking and eating. Instead, see it as an opportunity to experiment with new recipes and previously untried ingredients.

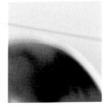

Allergy or Intolerance?

A food allergy occurs when the immune system overreacts to a normally harmless substance in a food by producing antibodies. This type of reaction often runs in families and can strike at any age. It may also cause a wide range of symptoms from a runny nose and headache to a potentially life-threatening reaction suffered by those who are allergic to nuts, for example.

Somewhat confusingly, if you test negatively for an allergy but still react to certain foods, then you may have what is controversially called an intolerance. An intolerance is often caused by a digestive problem.

What is a Gluten Allergy or Intolerance?

Gluten is a protein found in many cereal grains, including wheat, barley, rye, triticale, spelt, kamut and oats, and it is this substance that can cause a severe reaction in susceptible individuals. This reaction is known as coeliac disease. Coeliac disease is an inflammatory condition of the gastrointestinal tract. It is characterized by a flattening or wasting away of the villi – thread-like projections that line the intestines. The role of the villi is to absorb essential nutrients freed by the digestive process, and it is this process that is compromised in those with coeliac disease, causing among other symptoms malnutrition and weight loss.

Coeliac disease used to be rare and was once seen as a condition exclusive to childhood, but doctors now recognize that the disorder can affect people of all ages. While it may be present from birth and often runs in families, coeliac disease often remains undetected until adulthood. In the UK, about one in 1,000 people are believed to be affected by the life-long condition, yet this figure may be much higher due to many cases remaining undiagnosed.

What are the Symptoms?

The symptoms of coeliac disease are varied, ranging from a mild reaction to chronic illness, which can make diagnosis difficult. The most common symptoms include poor absorption of nutrients, particularly iron and folate, weight loss, mouth ulcers, nausea, bloating, extreme fatigue, lethargy, diarrhoea, flatulence and abdominal discomfort. In babies, coeliac disease will probably not become apparent until weaning, when gluten-containing foods are introduced. The infant will then typically develop pale, offensive-smelling stools, lethargy, vomiting, diarrhoea, irritability and a failure to grow properly.

How is it Diagnosed?

If gluten intolerance is suspected, a blood test is carried out to confirm the presence of antibodies and vitamin and mineral deficiencies. The blood tests are not 100 per cent accurate, so confirmation of a diagnosis is usually determined by a biopsy. This will generally be performed by a gastroenterologist in an outpatient clinic. A sample is taken from the lining of the small bowel using an endoscope, which will confirm the diagnosis of coeliac disease. It is recommended that you follow a normal diet containing gluten for six weeks prior to the blood test and biopsy to achieve accurate results.

What is the Treatment?

Once diagnosis has been confirmed, it is advisable to discuss the next step with a dietician or doctor before embarking on an elimination diet. The only treatment necessary to return the intestine to normal is to follow a strict gluten-free diet, eliminating the consumption of the cereal grains in question and any manufactured foods containing them, sometimes with a vitamin and mineral supplement. However, there is new research to suggest that some individuals may be able to tolerate small amounts of oats (less than 50 g/1 3/4 oz a day) in their diets, but it is advisable to consult your doctor or dietician before including oats in your diet and people with severe coeliac disease should avoid them altogether.

There are two forms of gluten foods: the first is the obvious bread, pasta, biscuits and pastries, while the second type relates to hidden gluten found in many manufactured foods. This could be wheat flour used as a binder or filler in foods as diverse as packet soups and bottled sauces. Those with coeliac disease need to become avid readers of nutritional information given on food labels to check for hidden sources of gluten.

What is a Wheat Allergy?

Wheat forms a major part of most people's diets, yet it is also a common allergen. The symptoms of wheat allergy or intolerance are varied and may include itchy, sore eyes; runny nose, sinusitis or sneezing; earache or ringing in the ears; headaches, migraine or dizziness; sore throats, bad breath, cough or mouth ulcers; skin rashes, acne, eczema or inexplicable bruising; stomach cramps, bloating, nausea, constipation or flatulence; as well as anxiety, depression, poor concentration or aggressive behaviour. Individuals who are allergic to wheat may be able to tolerate other grains, including those that contain gluten, such as rye, barley and oats.

Dermatitis Herpetiformis

This relatively rare skin disease is caused, like coeliac disease, by a sensitivity to gluten. It is characterized by an itchy rash that usually occurs on the elbows, buttocks and knees, although any area of the skin may be affected. Dermatitis herpetiformis is slightly more common in adult males than females and usually appears between the ages of 15 and 40, although it may occur at any age.

Am I Missing Out on Nutrients?

Before diagnosis, coeliacs have a problem absorbing nutrients from their diet, yet when gluten is excluded from the diet and as long as the sufferer eats a wide and varied diet, the body is in a better position to absorb nutrients from food. If you have cut out foods containing wheat and gluten, you may be concerned that you are not getting enough fibre. This is not a problem as long as you eat plenty of fruit and vegetables, other gluten-free grains, pulses, lentils and brown rice. Other nutrients found in wheat, barley, oats and rye include:

• zinc, found in nuts, seafood, oysters, wholegrains, pulses, seeds, liver and meat.

• vitamin B_1 (thiamine), found in wholegrains, nuts, pulses, meat and brewer's yeast.

• vitamin B_2 (riboflavin), found in eggs, yeast, green vegetables, pumpkin seeds and offal.

• vitamin B_3 (niacin), found in eggs, wholegrains, nuts, seafood, figs, prunes and offal.

• vitamin E, found in avocados, soya beans, dark green vegetables, eggs, nuts and vegetable oils.

What is a Dairy Allergy or Intolerance?

Dairy products, especially those derived from cow's milk, are a common allergen. Milk, cheese, cream, fromage frais, crème fraîche, yogurt and butter are obvious culprits, yet dairy products are found in many processed foods. A dairy allergy or intolerance usually manifests itself in childhood. A baby who is often sick, has colic or fails to thrive may be showing symptoms of a dairy allergy or intolerance, while weaning an infant too young may also encourage an allergic reaction. Thankfully, many children grow out of such allergies or intolerances by the age of five.

A reaction to dairy products is often due to lactose intolerance. This is when the body cannot produce an enzyme called lactase, which is necessary for the digestion of the natural sugar in milk, lactose. Those with lactose intolerance may be able to tolerate small amounts of dairy foods such as skimmed milk (rather than full-fat milk), yogurt or goat's milk, which are easier to digest. Although relatively unusual, some people may also be intolerant to the protein in dairy products, which causes similar side effects as lactose intolerance.

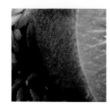

What are the Symptoms?

An allergy or intolerance to dairy products can provoke a wide range of symptoms, the most common being asthma, eczema, digestive problems, irritable bowel syndrome (IBS), rashes, sinus problems, including rhinitis, as well as migraines and headaches. If an individual does not produce the enzyme lactase, the lactose cannot be digested, which means that it passes unchanged into the large intestine where it is fermented by bacteria, causing bloating, stomach pains and diarrhoea. There is also growing evidence that child-onset diabetes is caused by dairy intolerance.

How is it Diagnosed?

It can be difficult to detect the presence of a dairy allergy or intolerance since symptoms may arise as soon as the problem food is eaten or may manifest themselves hours later. Symptoms may also vary depending on the individual. There are a number of tests now available to detect allergies,

including the RAST test, which measures the amount of immunoglobulin E antibodies (IgE) a person has to a specific substance, as well as the skin-prick test, whereby a small scratch is made by a pin carrying a suspect food and any reaction such as redness or swelling is monitored. Naturopaths also offer hair analysis and blood tests with varying success.

What is the Treatment?

A food exclusion diet, whereby offending foods are removed from the diet, is not only the most effective way of detecting the presence of a food intolerance or allergy but the most obvious way of eliminating symptoms. However, it can be a long and laborious process, which normally begins by keeping a detailed food diary. It is always important to consult a doctor or dietician before eliminating foods from your diet, who will be able to devise a nutritious, balanced, alternative diet.

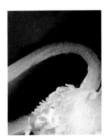

There are two forms of exclusion diet. The first relies on individuals suspecting which foods are causing a problem and eliminating them from their diet for a designated period of time to see if symptoms improve. The problem foods are then reintroduced to see if the symptoms recur. The second type of exclusion diet begins by eating a restricted diet based on a few foods that are highly unlikely to cause an allergic reaction. Foods are then reintroduced, one by one, on a gradual basis. If a food causes a reaction, it is subsequently eliminated from the diet. Obviously, this type of exclusion diet can take some time to complete.

Scientists are currently working on a new method of treating allergies or intolerances, but it is not as yet widely available. This involves administering tiny doses of an allergen with a naturally occurring enzyme through injection to desensitize its side effects. Those who are lactose intolerant may also take the enzyme lactase, which gives the body a helping hand in breaking down lactose in dairy foods.

When following a dairy exclusion diet, it is important to check the nutritional information on the labels of all foods and supplements before buying, since some artificial sweeteners and food supplements may also contain dairy-derived ingredients. Medicines can also have a dairy-derived content.

Am I Missing Out on Nutrients?

Milk and dairy products are a useful source of protein, zinc, calcium and vitamin B_{12}, so it is important to substitute these foods with others containing these nutrients. There are many non-dairy alternatives to milk that provide calcium, namely green leafy vegetables, sesame seeds, canned fish such as sardines and pilchards, white bread, apricots, baked beans, soya milk, molasses, nuts, seafood, cereals, seeds, pulses and soya products, while this group of foods also supplies valuable amounts of zinc. Vitamin B_{12} is provided by meat, fortified breakfast cereals, soya milk and yeast extract.

What Can I Eat?

If you are new to gluten-, wheat- and dairy-free cooking, understanding and remembering the ingredients that you can and can't eat can be quite daunting at first. It may require a total rethink of your repertoire of recipes and will undoubtedly demand a complete clear-out of your storecupboard, refrigerator and freezer. Try not to feel restricted or frightened by your new diet but regard it as the chance to explore a range of new foods, flavours and dishes. If catering for someone else, be reassured that cooking meals that are gluten-, wheat- and dairy-free is not difficult and they can be enjoyed by everyone in the family.

Checking the ingredients on food labels will need to become second nature, since a surprising number of foods contain wheat, gluten and dairy products, along with their derivatives. The most common dairy foods you need to avoid are cheese, cream, butter, milk, ice cream and yogurt. Foods such as pasta, noodles, bread, cakes, biscuits, pastries and pies are usually made with wheat, while barley, rye and oats also contain gluten. You will also need to watch out for canned soups, ready-prepared sauces and meals, as well as desserts, which may have added gluten or dairy products. Fillers, thickeners and binders are often wheat-based.

A Gluten-, Wheat- and Dairy-free Diet

Let's forget about what you can't eat and concentrate on the wide variety of delicious alternatives. If you eat a varied, balanced diet including the following food groups, you should get all the nutrients you need:

● Meat, fish, poultry or vegetarian alternatives

Fresh, frozen, cured and canned meat, fish and poultry are suitable but avoid those with a crumb coating or stuffing and check out processed pies, sausages and burgers. Some brands of meat-free sausages and burgers are suitable but double-check the label before buying. Tofu is a nutritious, low-fat, vegetarian source of protein.

● Fruit and vegetables

Fresh, frozen, dried or canned (in brine, juice, syrup, water or oil) are suitable. Potatoes make a useful alternative accompaniment to wheat-based foods such as pasta or noodles.

● Nuts and seeds

There is a wide range of ground, milled and whole nuts and seeds to choose from, which are an excellent source of protein as well as vitamins and minerals. Only buy from shops with a high turnover of stock to ensure freshness. Nut butters (cashew, peanut, hazelnut) are also suitable. Avoid dry-roasted nuts.

● Beans, pulses and lentils

Dried, fresh and canned (in brine, water or oil) beans, pulses and lentils are a low-fat source of protein, fibre, vitamins and minerals.

● Eggs

Avoid Scotch eggs due to their crumb coating.

● Drinks

Coffee, tea, herbal infusions, pure fruit juices and water are all suitable. Check cocoa powder, malted drinks, beer, spirits and wine for gluten, wheat and dairy additives.

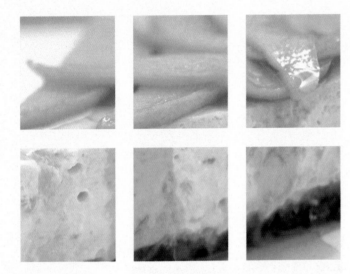

● Grains and cereals

There is now a wide range of alternatives to wheat and other gluten-containing grains, flakes and flours, including maize, buckwheat, millet, hominy grits, quinoa, sago, tapioca, rice, yam, gram or chickpea flour, polenta, arrowroot, cornflour, sorghum flour, potato flour, carob flour, teff flour, soya flour, sweet chestnut flour and yellow split pea flour. Breakfast cereals include some brands of cornflakes and muesli, puffed rice and rice crispies. For more information about the different types of grain, see below.

● Dairy-free alternatives

Soya, nut, rice, pea, quinoa and oat milk (some coeliacs may be able to tolerate the latter) are useful alternatives to dairy milk. Non-dairy soft and hard cheeses include alternatives to mozzarella, Edam, Gouda, Stilton, cream cheese, Parmesan and Cheddar. Soya yogurt, cream and ice cream are also available.

● Fats and oils

Look for dairy-free margarine (make sure it does not contain wheatgerm oil) and olive, vegetable and nut oils.

● Pasta and noodles

There is a wide range of gluten-, wheat- and dairy-free alternatives available made from corn, buckwheat, rice and millet flour, either used in combination or singly. Make sure that noodles and pasta do not contain added wheat flour, starch or binders.

● Chocolate and sweet foods

Look for plain dark, good-quality chocolate without added dairy products. Jams, honey, marmalade and maple syrup are all suitable.

● Gluten-free grains

There is a large variety of grains and cereals, whole, flaked or ground, to choose from that are both versatile and nutritious. The following are the most readily available gluten-free alternatives:

•Rice

This staple food for over half the world's population comes in many guises, from the sticky Japanese sushi rice to slender, fragrant basmati. For the gluten-free diet, this versatile grain offers a number of culinary possibilities, both sweet and savoury. It is impossible to create the perfect creamy risotto without using a specific type of fat, short-grain rice such as carnaroli or vialone nano, while Valencia rice is essential when making Spanish paella. Then there are rice flakes which can be added to muesli, biscuits and puddings; rice bran, a high-fibre addition to breads and cakes; as well as rice flour, often used to make sticky Asian cakes and sweets, and a common addition to gluten-free plain and self-raising flours.

•Buckwheat

Despite its name, buckwheat is not a type of wheat. The triangular-shaped grain is available toasted (kasha) or untoasted. The flour is used in Japan to make soba noodles, in Italy to make pasta and in Eastern Europe and Russia to make small pancakes called blinis. The flour has a greyish tinge and can be mixed with other kinds of gluten-free flour to give a lighter colour and texture. Buckwheat flakes make a nutritious addition to muesli. A complete protein, buckwheat also contains rutin, said to increase circulation and reduce high blood pressure.

•Millet

Known as the queen of grains, millet once rivalled barley as the staple food of Europe. It can be cooked in the same way as rice but is best dry-roasted first to enhance its mild flavour.

It is good served with stews or as a base for pilafs, porridge and milk puddings. The tiny, round grain can also be flaked or ground into flour. Millet has anti-fungal properties and is said to be good for candida overgrowth. It is also easily digested and beneficial for the stomach, spleen and pancreas.

•Quinoa

The 'mother grain' of the Incas, quinoa has the highest protein content of any grain, is very high in calcium and a good source of iron, B vitamins and vitamin E. The small, bead-like grains have a mild flavour and firm texture and make a good base for pilafs, bakes, tabbouleh (see page 35) and stuffings. It is cooked in the same way as rice. It can also be ground into flour or made into a milk.

•Amaranth

This much underrated grain contains more calcium than milk and is therefore useful for those on a dairy-free diet. Highly nutritious, amaranth is a tiny, pale grain with a strong, distinctive, nutty flavour. It can be used in stews and soups or ground into flour to make bread, cakes and pastries. Since it has an intense flavour, it is best combined with other more neutral flours and grains. Native to Mexico, amaranth is unusual in that its leaves can also be eaten cooked or raw.

•Maize

Also known as corn, this grain comes in yellow, blue, red and black varieties and is an indispensable addition to the gluten-free kitchen. It is a very versatile grain, with many uses. Cornmeal or polenta can be used to make bread, puddings, dumplings or a thick savoury porridge. Once cooked, polenta can be spread into an even layer, left to cool, then cut into slices and fried, grilled or griddled to make a base for bruschetta or it can be served as an accompaniment to soups and stews. Cornmeal comes in various grades, ranging from fine to coarse, which can take from 5–45 minutes to cook. Maize meal or 'masa harina' is made from the cooked whole grain, which is ground into flour and used to make the Mexican flat bread known as tortilla. Cornflour is a fine white powder and makes a useful thickener for sauces and soups.

Ready-made Gluten- and Wheat-free Foods

Many supermarkets now dedicate a special area to their range of gluten- and wheat-free foods, which may encompass anything from special flours, biscuits, breads, pizza bases and pasta to cakes, bread mixes, crispbreads and breakfast cereals. Mail order and healthfood shops are also a good source.

When using gluten-free flour (both plain and self-raising), it is important to follow the manufacturer's instructions since they don't necessarily perform in the same way as wheat flour.

Watch out for ...

Sources of wheat and gluten are not always easy to spot on food labels. If you notice any of the following, it is wise to check with the manufacturer: modified starch, wholegrain, starch, cereal, cereal protein, cornstarch, edible starch, food starch, binder, binding, vegetable protein, thickening or thickener, rusk and monosodium glutamate.

Also avoid ...

Wheat berries, wheat bran, wheat flour, bulgar wheat, durum wheat, couscous, semolina, seitan, wheatgerm, granary flour and bread, cracked wheat, pearl barley, barley flakes, pot barley, barley meal, rye in various forms, oats, oatmeal, oatgerm, pinhead oatmeal, oat bran, spelt, triticale and kamut.

Be aware ...

That the following may contain gluten: baking powder, gravy powder, spices, ready-ground pepper, shredded suet, mustard, stock powder and cubes, salad dressings, soy sauce (tamari is wheat-free), sausages, burgers, pies, ready-prepared meals, pâtés, crumb- or batter-coated fish and other foods, malt vinegar, yogurt, chilled desserts, cheese spreads, cornflakes, beer, malted-milk drinks and dry-roasted nuts.

Alternatives to Dairy Foods

It is now easy to find alternatives to the whole range of dairy products. The most widely available include:

● Soya

This is the most commonly used replacement for dairy milk and comes in many forms. Made from pulverized soya beans, soya milk is interchangeable with cow's milk, being suitable for both cooking and drinking. Soya milk comes both chilled and in long-life cartons. It may be sweetened, unsweetened, fortified with extra calcium and vitamins or flavoured with chocolate, banana or strawberry. Soya milk is also used to make cream, cheese, ice cream and yogurt. Soya cheese is made from a blend of processed soya beans and vegetable oils and may be flavoured with herbs and spices. There are also soya alternatives to Parmesan, Gouda, Cheddar and cream cheese. Other non-dairy cheeses include a Parmesan-type made from rice and another made from nuts and flavoured with spices.

Tofu is also made from soya beans and has little flavour of its own but readily absorbs other stronger flavours, making it extremely versatile. Firm tofu comes in a block and can be marinated, roasted, stewed or stir-fried. It is also available in a smoked form. Silken tofu has a softer texture and is used as

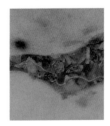

Watch out for ...

Sources of dairy products are not always easy to spot on food labels. If you notice any of the following, it is wise to check with the manufacturer: casein, hydrolysed casein, caseinate, albumen or albumin (may be sourced from eggs), lactic acid (E270), lactose, whey, non-fat milk solids, lacalbumin, skimmed milk powder, lactoglobulin and monosodium glutamate (MSG).

Also avoid ...

Cow's, goat's and sheep's milk, butter, soured cream, buttermilk, smetana, cream, fromage frais, yogurt, crème fraîche and ice cream.

Be aware ...

That the following may include dairy products: ready-prepared meals and desserts, pizza bases, sausages, pies, burgers, sauces, soups, ghee in Indian dishes (which may be clarified butter rather than being vegetable oil-based), wine, margarine, stock powder and cubes, biscuits, cakes, pâté, dips, chocolate and pastries.

an alternative to dairy cream or milk in desserts, sauces, dressings and soups. Other forms of tofu, which are now readily available, include smoked, marinated and deep fried. The latter is fairly tasteless but has an interesting texture and readily absorbs stonger flavours. Soya is a valuable source of calcium, iron, magnesium, phosphorus and vitamin E.

• Rice
Rice milk avoids the slightly 'floury' texture of soya milk and comes sweetened, unsweetened and fortified with calcium. It is easily digested and almost non-allergenic.

• Nut
Crushed and ground almonds or cashew nuts are mixed with water to make a versatile, mild-tasting milk. You can make your own by grinding nuts to a fine powder and blending with water. Add a banana and you have a delicious smoothie.

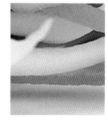

Breakfasts & Brunches

Numerous studies show that breakfast is an essential way to start the day, refuelling the body and providing much-needed sustained energy. For those avoiding gluten, wheat and dairy foods, breakfast need not be limited, as the following recipes demonstrate. There's a healthy apple muesli, which can be made in advance, a creamy smoothie for when time is short, as well as more substantial cooked brunches that are perfect for leisurely weekends.

serves 4

Berry & Yogurt Crunch

Ingredients

75 g/2³/₄ oz rice, buckwheat or millet flakes, or a mixture

4 tbsp clear honey

500 g/1 lb 2 oz thick natural soya yogurt or dairy-free alternative

finely grated rind of 1 orange

225 g/8 oz frozen mixed berries, partially thawed, plus extra to decorate

Nutritional Fact

Choose a yogurt with added 'beneficial bacteria' such as acidophilus or bifidobacteria – they can help to heal the gut and address food intolerances.

Serving Analysis

- Calories   198
- Protein   6g
- Carbohydrate   39g
- Sugars   22g
- Fat   3.5g
- Saturates   0.5g

1 Heat a dry frying pan over a medium heat, add the flakes and toast, shaking the pan, for 1 minute. Add half the honey and stir to coat the flakes. Cook, stirring constantly, until the flakes turn golden brown and slightly crisp.

2 Put the yogurt into a bowl and stir in the remaining honey and the orange rind. Gently stir in the berries, reserving a few to decorate. Leave for 10–15 minutes for the berries to release their juices, then stir again to give a swirl of colour.

3 To serve, spoon a layer of flakes into the bottom of 4 glasses, then top with a layer of the berry yogurt. Sprinkle with another layer of flakes and add another layer of the yogurt. Decorate with the reserved berries.

serves 4

Buckwheat Pancakes with Maple Syrup Bananas

Ingredients

50 g/1³/₄ oz buckwheat flour

50 g/1³/₄ oz gluten-free plain flour

pinch of salt

1 large egg, lightly beaten

125 ml/4 fl oz dairy-free milk

125 ml/4 fl oz water

40 g/1¹/₂ oz dairy-free margarine

For the maple syrup bananas

40 g/1¹/₂ oz dairy-free margarine

2 tbsp maple syrup

2 bananas, thickly sliced on the diagonal

1 Sift both types of flour and the salt into a mixing bowl. Make a well in the centre and add the beaten egg, milk and water. Using a balloon whisk, gradually mix the flour into the liquid ingredients, whisking well to get rid of any lumps, until you have a smooth batter.

2 Melt 25 g/1 oz of the margarine in a small saucepan and stir it into the batter. Pour the batter into a jug, cover and leave to rest for 30 minutes.

3 Melt half the remaining margarine in a medium-sized frying pan. When the pan is hot, pour in enough batter to make a thin pancake, swirling the pan to make an even layer.

4 Cook one side until lightly browned, then, using a palette knife, turn over and cook the other side. Slide on to a warm plate and cover with foil while you cook the remaining pancakes, adding more margarine when needed.

5 To make the maple syrup bananas, wipe the frying pan, add the margarine and heat until melted. Stir in the maple syrup, then add the bananas and cook for 2–3 minutes, or until the bananas have just softened and the sauce has thickened and caramelized. To serve, fold the pancakes in half and then half again, then top with bananas.

Nutritional Fact
Unusually for a plant-based food, buckwheat is a complete protein, containing all the essential amino acids. It also lowers blood cholesterol.

Serving Analysis

• Calories	339
• Protein	5.5g
• Carbohydrate	40g
• Sugars	13.5g
• Fat	19g
• Saturates	3.75g

serves 4

Millet Porridge with Apricot Purée

Ingredients

225 g/8 oz millet flakes

450 ml/16 fl oz dairy-free milk

pinch of salt

freshly grated nutmeg

For the apricot purée

115 g/4 oz no-soak dried apricots, roughly chopped

300 ml/10 fl oz water

Nutritional Fact

Millet is high in protein and is a rich source of B vitamins that you may miss when cutting out grains containing gluten.

Serving Analysis

• Calories   280

• Protein   10g

• Carbohydrate   49.5g

• Sugars   16.g

• Fat   4.75g

• Saturates   0.7g

1 To make the apricot purée, put the apricots into a saucepan and cover with the water. Bring to the boil, then reduce the heat and simmer, half covered, for 20 minutes until the apricots are very tender. Transfer the apricots, along with any water left in the saucepan, to a food processor or blender and process until smooth. Set aside.

2 To make the porridge, put the millet flakes into a saucepan and add the milk and salt. Bring to the boil, then reduce the heat and simmer for 5 minutes, stirring frequently, until cooked and creamy. To serve, spoon into 4 bowls and top with the apricot purée and a little nutmeg.

makes 10 portions

Apple Muesli

Ingredients

75 g/2³/₄ oz sunflower seeds
50 g/1³/₄ oz pumpkin seeds
90 g/3¹/₄ oz shelled hazelnuts, roughly chopped
125 g/4¹/₂ oz buckwheat flakes
125 g/4¹/₂ oz rice flakes
125 g/4¹/₂ oz millet flakes
115 g/4 oz no-soak dried apple, roughly chopped
115 g/4 oz dried stoned dates, roughly chopped

Nutritional Fact
Sunflower and pumpkin seeds contain essential omega oils that are vital for the health of the gut, skin and immune system.

Serving Analysis
- Calories   340
- Protein   8.7g
- Carbohydrate   48g
- Sugars   15g
- Fat   15g
- Saturates   1.75g

1 Heat a dry frying pan over a medium heat, add the seeds and hazelnuts and lightly toast, shaking the pan frequently, for 4 minutes, or until golden brown. Transfer to a large mixing bowl and leave to cool.

2 Add the flakes, apple and dates to the bowl and mix thoroughly until combined. Store the muesli in an airtight jar or container.

serves 3–4

Almond & Banana Smoothie

Ingredients

125 g/4 1/2 oz whole blanched almonds

600 ml/1 pint dairy-free milk

2 ripe bananas, halved

1 tsp natural vanilla extract

ground cinnamon, for sprinkling

1 Put the almonds into a food processor and process until very finely chopped. Add the milk, bananas and vanilla extract and blend until smooth and creamy. Pour into glasses and sprinkle with cinnamon.

Nutritional Fact
Almonds help to reduce cravings that often form part of an intolerance. They also help to reduce cholesterol.

Serving Analysis
- *Calories*   282
- *Protein*   10.4g
- *Carbohydrate*   22g
- *Sugars*   12.5g
- *Fat*   19g
- *Saturates*   1.9g

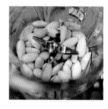

serves 3–4

Sausage & Potato Brunch

Ingredients

4 gluten-free sausages or vegetarian alternative

sunflower oil, for frying

4 boiled potatoes, cooled and diced

8 cherry tomatoes

4 eggs, beaten

salt and pepper

Nutritional Fact

Eggs are an excellent breakfast food as they contain sulphur, which helps the liver clear out waste products and toxins.

Serving Analysis

• Calories	435
• Protein	17g
• Carbohydrate	22g
• Sugars	2.5g
• Fat	30g
• Saturates	10.7g

1 Preheat the grill to medium-high. Arrange the sausages on a foil-lined grill pan and cook under the preheated grill, turning occasionally, for 12–15 minutes, or until cooked through and golden brown. Leave to cool slightly, then slice into bite-sized pieces.

2 Meanwhile, heat a little oil in a medium-sized (25-cm/10-inch), heavy-based frying pan with a heatproof handle over a medium heat. Add the potatoes and cook until golden brown and crisp all over, then add the tomatoes and cook for a further 2 minutes. Arrange the sausages in the pan so that there is an even distribution of potatoes, tomatoes and sausages.

3 Add a little more oil to the pan if it seems dry. Season the beaten eggs to taste and pour the mixture over the ingredients in the pan. Cook for 3 minutes, without stirring or disturbing the eggs. Place the pan under the preheated grill for 3 minutes, or until the top is just cooked. Cut into wedges to serve.

serves 4

Potato Cakes with Bacon & Maple Syrup

Ingredients

115 g/4 oz cold mashed potatoes

200 ml/7 fl oz dairy-free milk

75g /2³/₄ oz gluten-free self-raising flour

pinch of salt

1 egg, beaten

sunflower oil, for frying

To serve

8 good-quality bacon rashers, grilled until crisp

1¹/₂ tbsp maple syrup

Nutritional Fact
Starting the day with a hearty and substantial breakfast can help to ensure sustained energy release throughout the morning.

Serving Analysis
- Calories   217
- Protein   8.1g
- Carbohydrate   28g
- Sugars   5.3g
- Fat   9.3g
- Saturates   2.5g

1 Put the mashed potatoes and milk into a food processor or blender and process to a thin purée.

2 Sift the flour and salt into a mixing bowl, make a well in the centre of the flour and add the beaten egg and potato purée. Using a balloon whisk, gradually mix the flour into the liquid ingredients, whisking well to make a smooth, creamy, fairly thick batter.

3 Heat a little oil in a large, non-stick frying pan. Pour a small ladleful of batter per cake into the pan – you will probably fit about 3 in the pan at one time. Cook each cake for 2 minutes on each side until golden brown. Remove from the pan and keep warm while you cook the remaining potato cakes.

4 Divide the cakes between 4 warmed plates, top each serving with 2 bacon rashers and drizzle with maple syrup.

Soups & Light Meals

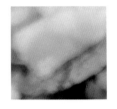

Warming, healthy and filling, the soups in this chapter

are simple to prepare and make use of readily available

ingredients. They can also be made in advance, making them

perfect for families who eat at varying times, enabling

everyone to enjoy the same nutritious meal. The recipes cater

for all eating occasions from the quick snack to the light

summery lunch but can also be turned into more substantial

meals when combined with other recipes in this book.

serves 4

Spicy Carrot & Lentil Soup

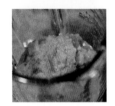

Ingredients

2 tbsp olive oil

1 large onion, chopped

1 celery stick, chopped

1 potato, diced

6 carrots, sliced

1 tsp paprika

2 tsp ground cumin

1 tsp ground coriander

$^1/_2$ tsp chilli powder (optional)

175 g/6 oz red split lentils

1.2 litres/2 pints vegetable or chicken stock

2 bay leaves

salt and pepper

2 tbsp chopped fresh coriander, to garnish

Nutritional Fact
Traditionally used to treat flatulence, cumin is known to aid digestion and improve circulation to the gastrointestinal tract.

Serving Analysis

- *Calories*   277
- *Protein*   13g
- *Carbohydrate*   40g
- *Sugars*   7g
- *Fat*   8.5g
- *Saturates*   0.25g

1 Heat the oil in a large, heavy-based saucepan over a medium-low heat. Add the onion and fry for 7 minutes, stirring occasionally. Add the celery, potato and carrots and cook for a further 5 minutes, stirring occasionally. Stir in the paprika, cumin, ground coriander and chilli powder, if using, and cook for a further minute.

2 Stir in the lentils, stock and bay leaves. Bring to the boil, then reduce the heat and simmer, half-covered, over a low heat, stirring occasionally to prevent the lentils sticking to the bottom of the saucepan, for 25 minutes, or until the lentils are tender.

3 Remove and discard the bay leaves. Transfer to a food processor or blender, or use a hand blender, and process the soup until thick and smooth. Return to the saucepan and reheat. Season to taste with salt and pepper and add extra chilli powder, if liked. Ladle into 4 warmed bowls and sprinkle with fresh coriander before serving.

serves 4

Roasted Red Onion Soup with Polenta Croûtons

Ingredients

800 g/1 lb 12 oz red onions, peeled and quartered

1 tbsp olive oil

15 g/¹/₂ oz dairy-free margarine

salt and pepper

250 ml/9 fl oz dry white wine

1.2 litres/2 pints vegetable stock

1 fresh rosemary sprig, plus extra to garnish

1 tsp chopped fresh thyme

1 tsp Dijon mustard

For the croûtons

300 ml/10 fl oz water

60 g/2¹/₄ oz fine instant polenta

¹/₂ tsp salt

1 tbsp chopped fresh rosemary

olive oil, for brushing

Nutritional Fact

Onions contain sulphur, which is a very important component of all body tissues, and may help to heal the gut, as well as protect against cancer.

Serving Analysis

• Calories	218
• Protein	3.2g
• Carbohydrate	22.5g
• Sugars	8.7g
• Fat	8.7g
• Saturates	0.6g

1 Preheat the oven to 200°C/400°F/Gas Mark 6. Put the onions and oil into a roasting tin and toss well. Dot with the margarine, season to taste with salt and roast in the preheated oven for 45 minutes, turning occasionally, until very tender and slightly blackened around the edges. Remove from the oven and leave to cool slightly.

2 Discard the outer layer of each onion segment if crisp, then cut the remainder into thick slices. Put the onions into a large, heavy-based saucepan with the wine and bring to the boil. Cook until most of the wine has evaporated and the smell of alcohol has disappeared.

3 Stir in the stock and herbs and cook over a medium-low heat for 30–35 minutes, or until reduced and thickened. Stir in the mustard and season to taste with salt and pepper.

4 Meanwhile, to make the polenta croûtons, heat the water to boiling point in a saucepan. Pour in the polenta in a steady stream and cook, stirring constantly with a wooden spoon, for 5 minutes, or until thickened and the mixture starts to come away from the sides of the saucepan. Stir in the salt and rosemary.

5 Cover a chopping board with a sheet of clingfilm, then, using a palette knife, spread out the polenta in an even layer about 1 cm/¹/₂ inch thick. Leave to cool and firm up. Cut into bite-sized cubes, brush with oil and arrange on a baking sheet. Cook in the oven, turning occasionally, for 10–15 minutes, or until crisp and lightly golden brown.

6 Remove and discard the rosemary from the soup. Transfer half the soup to a food processor or blender and process until smooth, then return to the saucepan and stir well. To serve, ladle into 4 warmed bowls and top with the polenta croûtons and sprigs of rosemary.

serves 4–6

Herby Potato Salad

Ingredients

500 g/1 lb 2 oz new potatoes

salt and pepper

16 vine-ripened cherry tomatoes, halved

70 g/2^1/$_2$ oz black olives, stoned and coarsely chopped

4 spring onions, finely sliced

2 tbsp chopped fresh mint

2 tbsp chopped fresh parsley

2 tbsp chopped fresh coriander

juice of 1 lemon

3 tbsp extra virgin olive oil

1 Cook the potatoes in a saucepan of lightly salted boiling water for 15 minutes, or until tender. Drain, then leave to cool slightly before peeling off the skins. Cut into halves or quarters, depending on the size of the potato. Then combine with the tomatoes, olives, spring onions and herbs in a salad bowl.

2 Mix the lemon juice and oil together in a small bowl or jug and pour over the potato salad. Season to taste with salt and pepper before serving.

Nutritional Fact

Parsley can help ease food intolerances by assisting the adrenal glands. Overworked adrenals mean that energy and nutrients that could help deal with intolerances are diverted from the gut.

Serving Analysis

- Calories   202
- Protein   2.5g
- Carbohydrate   25.5g
- Sugars   2.8g
- Fat   11.2g
- Saturates   0.06g

serves 4

Tabbouleh

Ingredients

175 g/6 oz quinoa

600 ml/1 pint water

10 vine-ripened cherry tomatoes, deseeded and chopped

7.5-cm/3-inch piece cucumber, diced

3 spring onions, finely chopped

juice of 1/2 lemon

2 tbsp extra virgin olive oil

4 tbsp chopped fresh mint

4 tbsp chopped fresh coriander

4 tbsp chopped fresh parsley

salt and pepper

Nutritional Fact
The super-nutritious grain quinoa is used here instead of the usual bulgar wheat or couscous to make this filling salad. It is at its most flavourful when served at room temperature.

Serving Analysis
* *Calories*   283
* *Protein*   8.3g
* *Carbohydrate*   43g
* *Sugars*   6.8g
* *Fat*   10.4g
* *Saturates*   0.38g

1 Put the quinoa into a medium-sized saucepan and cover with the water. Bring to the boil, then reduce the heat, cover and simmer over a low heat for 15 minutes. Drain if necessary.

2 Leave the quinoa to cool slightly before combining with the remaining ingredients in a salad bowl. Season to taste with salt and pepper before serving.

serves 4

Walnut, Pear & Crispy Bacon Salad

Ingredients

4 lean bacon rashers

75 g/2³/₄ oz walnut halves

2 Red William pears, cored and sliced lengthways

1 tbsp lemon juice

175 g/6 oz watercress, tough stalks removed

For the dressing

3 tbsp extra virgin olive oil

2 tbsp lemon juice

¹/₂ tsp clear honey

salt and pepper

Nutritional Fact

Watercress contains good levels of beta-carotene and lutein, plant chemicals that give it its colour and help to support the immune system.

Serving Analysis

• Calories	433
• Protein	6.3g
• Carbohydrate	18g
• Sugars	11.8g
• Fat	39.5g
• Saturates	1g

1 Preheat the grill to high. Arrange the bacon on a foil-lined grill pan and cook under the preheated grill until well-browned and crisp. Set aside to cool, then cut into 1-cm/¹/₂-inch pieces.

2 Meanwhile, heat a dry frying pan over a medium heat and lightly toast the walnuts, shaking the pan frequently, for 3 minutes, or until lightly browned. Set aside to cool.

3 Toss the pears in the lemon juice to prevent discolouration. Put the watercress, walnuts, pears and bacon into a salad bowl.

4 To make the dressing, whisk the oil, lemon juice and honey together in a small bowl or jug. Season to taste with salt and pepper, then pour over the salad. Toss well to combine and serve.

serves 2 as a main course or 4 as a starter

Buckwheat Noodle Salad with Smoked Tofu

Ingredients

200 g/7 oz buckwheat noodles

250 g/9 oz firm smoked tofu (drained weight)

200 g/7 oz white cabbage, finely shredded

250 g/9 oz carrots, finely shredded

3 spring onions, diagonally sliced

1 fresh red chilli, deseeded and finely sliced into rounds

2 tbsp sesame seeds, lightly toasted

For the dressing

1 tsp grated fresh root ginger

1 garlic clove, crushed

175 g/6 oz silken tofu (drained weight)

4 tsp tamari (wheat-free soy sauce)

2 tbsp sesame oil

4 tbsp hot water

salt

Nutritional Fact

Cabbage is a member of the brassica family, along with broccoli, cauliflower, kale and Brussels sprouts, which all aid liver function.

Serving Analysis

• Calories	326
• Protein	16g
• Carbohydrate	50g
• Sugars	4g
• Fat	9g
• Saturates	1g

1 Cook the noodles in a large saucepan of lightly salted boiling water according to the packet instructions. Drain and refresh under cold running water.

2 To make the dressing, blend the ginger, garlic, silken tofu, soy sauce, oil and water together in a small bowl until smooth and creamy. Season to taste with salt.

3 Place the smoked tofu in a steamer. Steam for 5 minutes, then cut into thin slices.

4 Meanwhile, put the cabbage, carrots, spring onions and chilli into a bowl and toss to mix. To serve, arrange the noodles on serving plates and top with the carrot salad and slices of tofu. Spoon over the dressing and sprinkle with sesame seeds.

serves 4–6

Baba Ghanoush with Flat Breads

Ingredients

1 large aubergine, pricked all over with a fork

3 fat garlic cloves, unpeeled

1 tsp ground coriander

1 tsp ground cumin

1 tbsp light tahini

juice of 1/2 lemon

2 tbsp extra virgin olive oil

salt and pepper

coriander, to garnish

For the flat breads

250 g/9 oz gluten-free strong white flour

2 tbsp fine cornmeal or polenta

1 tsp gluten-free baking powder

1 tsp salt

50 g/1 3/4 oz dairy-free margarine, diced

1 tbsp sesame seeds (optional)

150–175 ml/5–6 fl oz warm water

sunflower oil, for oiling

1 To make the baba ghanoush, preheat the oven to 200°C/ 400°F/Gas Mark 6. Put the aubergine into a roasting tin and bake in the preheated oven for 25 minutes. Add the garlic cloves to the tin and cook for a further 15 minutes until the aubergine and garlic are very tender.

2 Halve the aubergine and scoop out the flesh with a spoon into a food processor or blender. Peel the garlic cloves and add to the food processor or blender with the spices, tahini, lemon juice and oil. Process until smooth and creamy, then season to taste with salt and pepper. Transfer to a serving dish and cover until required.

3 Meanwhile, make the flat breads. Sift the flour, cornmeal, baking powder and salt into a mixing bowl, then rub in the margarine with your fingertips until the mixture resembles breadcrumbs. Add the sesame seeds, if using, and stir in the water, first with a wooden spoon, then with your hands to bring the mixture together into a ball, adding more water or flour as necessary.

4 Turn the mixture out on to a lightly floured work surface and knead lightly until a soft dough forms. Divide into 6 pieces, then roll each piece into a ball. Wrap in clingfilm and leave to rest in the refrigerator for 30 minutes.

5 Roll out or press the dough balls with your fingers into 5-mm/1/4-inch thick rounds – it is quite crumbly and fragile, so don't worry if the edges are slightly rough. Heat a lightly oiled griddle pan over a medium heat and cook each flat bread for a few minutes on each side until lightly golden, keeping them warm while you finish cooking the remainder. Serve warm with the baba ghanoush.

Nutritional Fact

Garlic is a potent natural antibiotic, which can help to keep the gut clear of the microbes that can contribute to digestive problems.

Serving Analysis

- *Calories*   377
- *Protein*   6g
- *Carbohydrate*   51g
- *Sugars*   3.2g
- *Fat*   18g
- *Saturates*   2g

makes 16 rolls

Vietnamese Rolls with Caramelized Pork & Noodles

Ingredients

2 tbsp tamari (wheat-free soy sauce)

1 1/2 tsp maple syrup

500 g/1 lb 2 oz lean pork fillets

vegetable oil, for frying

32 rice paper pancakes

70 g/2 1/2 oz rice vermicelli noodles, cooked

To serve

gluten-free hoisin sauce

strips of cucumber

strips of spring onion

Nutritional Fact

Fermented soy (found in tamari) is good for liver function. When our hormones are out of balance, the liver has to work hard processing these extra hormones. Since soy can help to balance hormones, the liver has a lighter load.

Serving Analysis

• Calories	109
• Protein	7g
• Carbohydrate	8g
• Sugars	0.7g
• Fat	5g
• Saturates	0.08g

1 Blend the tamari and maple syrup together in a shallow dish. Add the pork and turn to coat in the mixture. Cover and leave to marinate in the refrigerator for at least 1 hour or preferably overnight.

2 Heat a griddle pan over a medium-high heat until hot, add a little oil to cover the base and cook the pork for 4–6 minutes each side, depending on the thickness of the fillets, until cooked and caramelized on the outside. Remove from the pan and slice into fine strips.

3 Fill a heatproof bowl with water that is just off the boil. Put 2 rice paper pancakes on top of one another (you will need 2 per roll as they are very thin and fragile) and soak in the water for 20 seconds, or until they turn pliable and opaque. Carefully remove using a spatula, drain for a second and place flat on a plate.

4 Spread a spoonful of hoisin sauce over the pancake and top with a small bundle of noodles and a few strips of pork, cucumber and spring onion. Fold in the ends and sides of the pancake to resemble a spring roll. Set aside while you make the remaining rolls. Slice in half on the diagonal and serve with a little more hoisin sauce, if liked.

serves 2 as a main course or 4 as a starter

Mixed Sushi Rolls

1 Put the rice into a saucepan and cover with cold water. Bring to the boil, then reduce the heat, cover and simmer for 15–20 minutes, or until the rice is tender and the water has been absorbed. Drain if necessary and transfer to a bowl. Mix the vinegar, sugar and salt together, then, using a spatula, stir well into the rice. Cover with a damp cloth and leave to cool.

2 To make the rolls, lay a clean bamboo mat over a chopping board. Lay a sheet of nori, shiny side-down, on the mat. Spread a quarter of the rice mixture over the nori, using wet fingers to press it down evenly, leaving a 1-cm/1/2-inch margin at the top and bottom.

3 For smoked salmon and cucumber rolls, lay the salmon over the rice and arrange the cucumber in a line across the centre. For the prawn rolls, lay the prawns and avocado in a line across the centre.

4 Carefully hold the nearest edge of the mat, then, using the mat as a guide, roll up the nori tightly to make a neat tube of rice enclosing the filling. Seal the uncovered edge with a little water, then roll the sushi off the mat. Repeat to make 3 more rolls – you need 2 salmon and cucumber and 2 prawn and avocado in total.

5 Using a wet knife, cut each roll into 8 pieces and stand upright on a platter. Wipe and rinse the knife between cuts to prevent the rice from sticking. Serve the rolls with wasabi, tamari and pickled ginger.

Ingredients

4 sheets nori (seaweed) for rolling

For the rice

250 g/9 oz sushi rice

2 tbsp rice vinegar

1 tsp caster sugar

1/2 tsp salt

For the fillings

50 g/1 3/4 oz smoked salmon

4-cm/1 1/2-inch piece cucumber, peeled, deseeded and cut into matchsticks

40 g/1 1/2 oz cooked peeled prawns

1 small avocado, stoned, peeled, thinly sliced and tossed in lemon juice

To serve

wasabi (Japanese horseradish sauce)

tamari (wheat-free soy sauce)

pink pickled ginger

Nutritional Fact

Nori is the seaweed with the most amount of protein. It also helps to rid the body of toxic metals.

Serving Analysis

• Calories	195
• Protein	7.5g
• Carbohydrate	23g
• Sugars	3.6g
• Fat	8.4g
• Saturates	1.4g

Seafood, Meat & Poultry

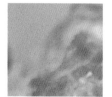    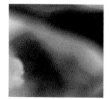 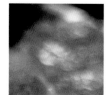

Inspired by a cross-section of cultures and flavours, this chapter features fragrant Malaysian-style coconut noodles with prawns, Italian pasta with a meatball sauce and a creamy southern Indian chicken curry, while travelling closer to home, there's a hearty beef stew with herby dumplings – all without a trace of gluten, wheat or dairy.

     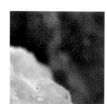

serves 4–6

Smoked Haddock & Prawn Flan

Ingredients

400 g/14 oz undyed smoked haddock or cod fillet, rinsed and dried

300 ml/10 fl oz dairy-free milk

150 g/5¹/₂ oz cooked peeled prawns

200 g/7 oz vegan cream cheese

3 eggs, beaten

3 tbsp snipped fresh chives

pepper

For the pastry

200 g/7 oz gluten-free plain flour

large pinch of salt

100 g/3¹/₂ oz dairy-free margarine, diced, plus extra for greasing

1 egg yolk

3 tbsp ice-cold water

1 Preheat the oven to 200°C/400°F/Gas Mark 6. Lightly grease a 26-cm/10¹/₂-inch flan dish.

2 To make the pastry, sift the flour and salt into a mixing bowl, then rub in the margarine with your fingertips until the mixture resembles coarse breadcrumbs. Stir in the egg yolk, followed by the water, then bring the mixture together into a ball. Turn out on to a lightly floured work surface and knead until smooth. Wrap in clingfilm and chill in the refrigerator for 30 minutes.

3 Meanwhile, put the fish into a shallow saucepan with the milk. Heat gently until simmering and simmer for 10 minutes, or until just cooked and opaque. Remove the fish with a slotted spoon, leave to cool a little, then peel away the skin and discard any bones. Flake the fish into large chunks and set aside. Reserve 125 ml/4 fl oz of the cooking liquid.

4 Roll out the pastry and use to line the prepared flan dish. Line the pastry case with baking paper and dried beans and bake in the preheated oven for 8 minutes. Remove the paper and beans and bake for a further 5 minutes.

5 Arrange the fish and prawns in the pastry case. Beat together the cream cheese, reserved cooking liquid, eggs, chives and pepper to taste in a bowl, then pour over the seafood. Bake for 30 minutes, or until the filling is set and golden brown.

Nutritional Fact

Haddock and cod contain good amounts of vitamin A, which helps to heal the gut lining, a very important part of addressing food intolerances.

Serving Analysis

- Calories   592
- Protein   34g
- Carbohydrate   34g
- Sugars   1g
- Fat   35.5g
- Saturates   8.7g

serves 4

Baked Lemon Cod with Herb Sauce

Ingredients

4 thick cod fillets

olive oil, for brushing

8 thin lemon slices

salt and pepper

For the herb sauce

4 tbsp olive oil

1 garlic clove, crushed

4 tbsp chopped fresh parsley

2 tbsp chopped fresh mint

juice of $^1/_2$ lemon

salt and pepper

Nutritional Fact

Olive oil remains relatively stable when heated and is therefore good for cooking. It has been shown to reduce cholesterol levels.

Serving Analysis

- *Calories*   *232*
- *Protein*   *21g*
- *Carbohydrate*   *2g*
- *Sugars*   *0.2g*
- *Fat*   *16g*
- *Saturates*   *0.1g*

1 Preheat the oven to 200°C/400°F/Gas Mark 6. Rinse each cod fillet and pat dry with kitchen paper, then brush with oil. Place each fillet on a piece of baking paper that is large enough to encase the fish in a parcel. Top each fillet with 2 lemon slices and season to taste with salt and pepper. Fold over the baking paper to encase the fish and bake in the preheated oven for 20 minutes, or until just cooked and opaque.

2 Meanwhile, to make the herb sauce, put all the ingredients into a food processor and process until finely chopped. Season to taste with salt and pepper.

3 Carefully unfold each parcel and place on serving plates. Pour a spoonful of herb sauce over each piece of fish before serving.

serves 4

Malaysian-style Coconut Noodles with Prawns

Ingredients

2 tbsp vegetable oil

1 small red pepper, deseeded and diced

200 g/7 oz pak choi, stalks thinly sliced and leaves chopped

2 large garlic cloves, chopped

1 tsp ground turmeric

2 tsp garam masala

1 tsp chilli powder (optional)

125 ml/4 fl oz hot vegetable stock

2 heaped tbsp smooth peanut butter

350 ml/12 fl oz coconut milk

1 tbsp tamari (wheat-free soy sauce)

250 g/9 oz thick rice noodles

280 g/10 oz cooked peeled large prawns

 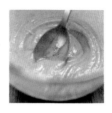 

To garnish

2 spring onions, finely shredded

1 tbsp sesame seeds

Nutritional Fact

Like mother's milk, coconut milk contains lauric acid, which protects against viruses and bacterial infections.

Serving Analysis

• Calories	428
• Protein	20g
• Carbohydrate	31g
• Sugars	10g
• Fat	26g
• Saturates	7g

1 Heat the oil in a wok or large, heavy-based frying pan over a high heat. Add the red pepper, pak choi stalks and garlic and stir-fry for 3 minutes. Add the turmeric, garam masala, chilli powder, if using, and pak choi leaves and stir-fry for a further minute.

2 Mix the hot stock and peanut butter together in a heatproof bowl until the peanut butter has dissolved, then add to the stir-fry with the coconut milk and tamari. Cook for 5 minutes over a medium heat, or until reduced and thickened.

3 Meanwhile, immerse the noodles in a bowl of just boiled water. Leave for 4 minutes, then drain and refresh the noodles under cold running water. Add the cooked noodles and prawns to the coconut curry and cook for a further 2–3 minutes, stirring frequently, until heated through.

4 Serve the noodle dish sprinkled with spring onions and sesame seeds.

serves 2–3

Salmon Fingers with Potato Wedges

Ingredients

150 g/5 oz fine cornmeal or polenta

1 tsp paprika

400 g/14 oz salmon fillet, skinned and sliced into 12 chunky fingers

1 egg, beaten

sunflower oil, for frying

salt and pepper

For the potato wedges

500 g/1 lb 2 oz potatoes, scrubbed and cut into thick wedges

1–2 tbsp olive oil

$1/2$ tsp paprika

salt

Nutritional Fact

Salmon is an oily fish, high in omega-3 fatty acids, which help to protect the brain, eyes, heart and liver.

Serving Analysis
- Calories   665
- Protein   35g
- Carbohydrate   73g
- Sugars   2g
- Fat   27g
- Saturates   4g

1 Preheat the oven to 200°C/400°F/Gas Mark 6. To make the chips, dry the potato wedges on a clean tea towel. Spoon the oil into a roasting tin and put into the preheated oven briefly to heat. Toss the potatoes in the warm oil until well coated. Sprinkle with paprika and salt to taste and roast for 30 minutes, turning halfway through, until crisp and golden.

2 Meanwhile, mix the cornmeal and paprika together on a plate. Dip each salmon finger into the beaten egg, then roll in the cornmeal mixture until evenly coated.

3 Heat enough oil to cover the base of a large, heavy-based frying pan over a medium heat. Carefully arrange half the salmon fingers in the pan and cook for 6 minutes, turning halfway through, until golden. Drain on kitchen paper and keep warm while you cook the remaining fingers. Serve with the potato wedges.

Nutritional Fact

Beef is a great source of iron, which is much more readily absorbed in the form found in meat rather than in plant sources.

Serving Analysis

- Calories   819
- Protein   38g
- Carbohydrate   35.5g
- Sugars   3.3g
- Fat   58g
- Saturates   20.4g

serves 4

Winter Beef Stew with Herb Dumplings

Ingredients

3 tbsp gluten-free plain flour

salt and pepper

800 g/1 lb 12 oz braising steak, cubed

3 tbsp olive oil

12 shallots, peeled and halved, or
quartered if large

2 carrots, cut into batons

1 parsnip, sliced into rounds

2 bay leaves

1 tbsp chopped fresh rosemary

475 ml/16 fl oz cider

250 ml/8½ fl oz beef stock

1 tbsp tamari (wheat-free soy sauce)

200 g/7 oz canned chestnuts, drained

For the herb dumplings

115 g/4 oz gluten-free self-raising
flour, plus extra for flouring

50 g/1¾ oz gluten-free vegetable suet

2 tbsp chopped fresh thyme

salt and pepper

1 Preheat the oven to 160°C/325°F/Gas Mark 3. Put the flour into a clean polythene bag or on a plate and season generously with salt and pepper. Toss the beef in the seasoned flour until coated.

2 Heat 1 tablespoon of the oil in a large, flameproof casserole dish over a medium-high heat. Add one-third of the beef and cook for 5–6 minutes, turning occasionally, until browned all over – the meat may stick to the pan until it is properly sealed. Remove the beef with a slotted spoon. Cook the remaining 2 batches, adding another tablespoon of oil as necessary. Set aside when all the beef has been sealed.

3 Add the remaining oil to the pan with the shallots, carrots, parsnip and herbs and cook for 3 minutes, stirring occasionally. Pour in the cider and beef stock and bring to the boil. Cook over a high heat until the alcohol has evaporated and the liquid reduced. Add the stock and tamari, then cook for a further 3 minutes.

4 Stir in the chestnuts and beef, cover and cook in the preheated oven for 1 hour 35 minutes.

5 Meanwhile, to make the dumplings, combine all the ingredients in a bowl and season to taste with salt and pepper. Mix in enough water to make a soft dough. Divide the dough into walnut-sized pieces and, using floured hands, roll each piece into a ball.

6 Add to the casserole dish, cover and cook for a further 25 minutes, or until the dumplings are cooked, the stock has formed a thick, rich gravy and the meat is tender. Season to taste with salt and pepper before serving.

serves 4

Pasta with Italian Meatball Sauce

Ingredients

300 g/10¹/₂ oz dried gluten-free spaghetti

salt and pepper

For the meatballs

40 g/1¹/₂ oz fresh gluten-free breadcrumbs

450 g/1 lb fresh lean beef mince

1 onion, grated

1 large garlic clove, crushed

1 egg, beaten

salt and pepper

For the tomato sauce

1 tbsp olive oil

2 garlic cloves, chopped

2 tsp dried oregano

300 ml/10 fl oz dry white wine

600 ml/1 pint passata

1 bay leaf

2 tsp tomato purée

¹/₂ tsp sugar

Nutritional Fact

Tomatoes are rich in an antioxidant called lycopene, which helps immune function and gut healing.

Serving Analysis

• Calories	732
• Protein	36g
• Carbohydrate	87g
• Sugars	10g
• Fat	21g
• Saturates	5.3g

1 To make the meatballs, put the breadcrumbs, mince, onion, garlic and egg into a bowl and mix well until combined. Season to taste with salt and pepper, cover and chill in the refrigerator for 30 minutes.

2 Meanwhile, make the tomato sauce. Heat the oil in a large, heavy-based frying pan over a medium heat and fry the garlic, stirring, for 1 minute. Add the oregano and cook, stirring, for a further minute. Pour in the wine and cook over a high heat until it has almost evaporated.

3 Add the passata, bay leaf, tomato purée and sugar, then stir well. Partially cover the pan and cook over a medium-low heat for 5 minutes.

4 Form the meatball mixture into walnut-sized balls. Add to the sauce, partially cover and cook for 15–20 minutes, or until the meatballs are cooked through.

5 Meanwhile, cook the pasta in a large saucepan of lightly salted boiling water according to the packet instructions. Drain, reserving 3 tablespoons of the cooking liquid. Stir the cooking liquid into the sauce before serving with the pasta.

serves 4

Lamb Koftas with Chickpea Mash

Ingredients

250 g/9 oz fresh lean lamb mince

1 onion, finely chopped

1 tbsp chopped fresh coriander

1 tbsp chopped fresh parsley

1/2 tsp ground coriander

1/4 tsp chilli powder

salt and pepper

For the chickpea mash

1 tbsp olive oil

2 garlic cloves, chopped

400 g/14 oz canned chickpeas, drained and rinsed

50 ml/2 fl oz dairy-free milk

salt and pepper

2 tbsp chopped fresh coriander

Nutritional Fact

Chickpeas, like all legumes, are high in soluble fibre, which helps to clean out the gut by absorbing and eliminating toxins via the bowel.

Serving Analysis

- Calories 349
- Protein 21g
- Carbohydrate 19g
- Sugars 1.7g
- Fat 21g
- Saturates 5.1g

1 Put the lamb, onion, herbs, spices and salt and pepper to taste in a food processor. Process until thoroughly combined.

2 Divide the mixture into 8 portions and, using wet hands, shape each portion into a sausage shape around a wooden skewer (soaked in water first to prevent burning). Cover and chill the skewers in the refrigerator for 30 minutes.

3 To cook, preheat a griddling pan over a medium heat and brush with a little oil. Cook the skewers in 2 batches, turning occasionally, for 10 minutes, or until browned on all sides and cooked through.

4 To make the chickpea mash, heat the oil in a saucepan and gently fry the garlic for 2 minutes. Add the chickpeas and milk and heat through for a few minutes. Transfer to a food processor or blender and process until smooth. Season to taste with salt and pepper, then stir in the fresh coriander. Serve the mash with the koftas.

serves 4

Creamy Chicken Curry with Lemon Rice

Ingredients

2 tbsp vegetable oil

4 skinless, boneless chicken breasts, about 800 g/1 lb 12 oz in total, cut into 2.5-cm/1-inch pieces

1 1/2 tsp cumin seeds

1 large onion, grated

2 fresh green chillies, finely chopped

2 large garlic cloves, grated

1 tbsp grated fresh root ginger

1 tsp ground turmeric

1 tsp ground coriander

1 tsp garam masala

300 ml/10 fl oz coconut milk

250 ml/9 fl oz canned chopped tomatoes

2 tsp lemon juice

salt

2 tbsp chopped fresh coriander, to garnish

 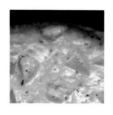 

For the lemon rice

350 g/12 oz basmati rice, rinsed

1.2 litres/2 pints water

juice and grated rind of 1 lemon

3 cloves

1 Heat the oil in a large, heavy-based saucepan over a medium heat. Add the chicken and cook for 5–8 minutes, turning frequently, until lightly browned and cooked through. Remove from the saucepan and set aside. Add the cumin seeds and cook until they begin to darken and sizzle. Stir in the onion, partially cover and cook over a medium-low heat, stirring frequently, for 10 minutes, or until soft and golden. Add the chillies, garlic, ginger, turmeric, ground coriander and garam masala and cook for 1 minute.

2 Return the chicken to the saucepan and stir in the coconut milk and tomatoes. Partially cover and cook over a medium heat for 15 minutes until the sauce has reduced and thickened. Stir in the lemon juice and season to taste with salt.

3 Meanwhile, make the rice. Put the rice into a saucepan and cover with the water. Add the lemon juice and cloves. Bring to the boil, then reduce the heat, cover and simmer over a very low heat for 15 minutes, or until the rice is tender and all the water has been absorbed. Remove the saucepan from the heat and stir in the lemon rind. Leave the rice to stand, covered, for 5 minutes.

4 Serve the curry with the lemon rice, sprinkled with fresh coriander.

Nutritional Fact

A potent anti-inflammatory, ginger has been used for centuries to treat stomach upsets, nausea, heartburn, abdominal cramps and travel sickness.

Serving Analysis

• *Calories*	*545*
• *Protein*	*46g*
• *Carbohydrate*	*29g*
• *Sugars*	*5.9g*
• *Fat*	*27g*
• *Saturates*	*6.8g*

serves 4

Roasted Chicken with Sun-blush Tomato Pesto

Ingredients

4 skinless, boneless chicken breasts, about 800 g/1 lb 12 oz in total

1 tbsp olive oil

salt and pepper

For the Pesto

125 g/4½ oz sun-blush tomatoes in oil (drained weight), chopped

2 garlic cloves, crushed

6 tbsp pine kernels, lightly toasted

150 ml/5 fl oz extra virgin olive oil

1 Preheat the oven to 200°C/400°F/Gas Mark 6. To make the red pesto, put the sun-blush tomatoes, garlic, 4 tablespoons of the pine kernels and oil into a food processor and process to a coarse paste.

2 Arrange the chicken in a large, ovenproof dish or roasting tin. Brush each breast with the oil, then place a tablespoon of red pesto over each breast. Using the back of a spoon, spread the pesto so that it covers the top of each breast. This pesto recipe makes more than just the four tablespoons used here. Store the extra pesto in an airtight container in the refrigerator for up to 1 week.

3 Roast the chicken in the preheated oven for 30 minutes, or until tender and the juices run clear when a skewer is inserted into the thickest part of the meat.

4 Serve sprinkled with the remaining toasted pine kernels.

Nutritional Fact

Pine kernels are nuts with a high protein content and also vitamin E, both of which help to repair structures in the gut.

Serving Analysis

• Calories	558
• Protein	21g
• Carbohydrate	9.5g
• Sugars	0.5g
• Fat	51g
• Saturates	2.1g

 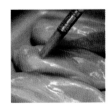 

Vegetarian

 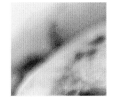    

For those who avoid meat, poultry or fish, or simply want to cut down on the amount they eat, this collection of appetizing and nourishing dishes is sure to inspire. The emphasis is on simple ingredients, including plenty of healthy vegetables, used in imaginative ways such as the North African aubergine tagine with polenta mash, Thai tofu cakes with a zingy sweet chilli dip, along with a classic Spanish tortilla.

  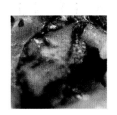 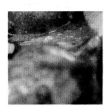 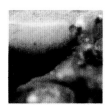 

serves 4

Rösti with Roasted Vegetables

1 For the roasted vegetables, mix the oil, vinegar and honey together in a large, shallow dish. Add the red pepper, courgettes, onions, fennel, tomatoes, garlic and rosemary to the dish and toss in the marinade. Leave to marinate for at least 1 hour.

2 Preheat the oven to 200°C/400°F/Gas Mark 6. Cook the potatoes in a saucepan of lightly salted boiling water for 8–10 minutes, or until partially cooked. Leave to cool, then coarsely grate.

3 Transfer the vegetables, except the tomatoes and garlic, and the marinade to a roasting tin. Roast in the preheated oven for 25 minutes, then add the tomatoes and garlic and roast for a further 15 minutes, or until the vegetables are tender and slightly blackened around the edges.

4 Meanwhile, cook the rösti. Take a quarter of the potato mixture in your hands and form into a roughly shaped cake. Heat just enough oil to cover the base of a frying pan over a medium heat. Put the cakes, 2 at a time, into the pan and flatten with a spatula to form rounds about 2 cm/³⁄₄ inch thick.

5 Cook the rösti for 6 minutes on each side, or until golden brown and crisp. Mix the dressing ingredients. To serve, top each rösti with the roasted vegetables and drizzle with a little pesto dressing. Season to taste.

Ingredients

900 g/2 lb potatoes, halved if large

salt

sunflower oil, for frying

For the vegan pesto dressing

2 tbsp vegan pesto

1 tbsp boiling water

1 tbsp extra virgin olive oil

For the roasted vegetables

2 tbsp extra virgin olive oil

1 tbsp balsamic vinegar

1 tsp clear honey

1 red pepper, deseeded and quartered

2 courgettes, sliced lengthways

2 red onions, quartered

1 small fennel bulb, cut into thin wedges

16 vine-ripened tomatoes

8 garlic cloves

2 fresh rosemary sprigs

salt and pepper

Nutritional Fact
Rosemary contains fat-soluble antioxidants that reduce the free radicals produced when oil is heated.

Serving Analysis
- *Calories* 447
- *Protein* 9g
- *Carbohydrate* 74g
- *Sugars* 19g
- *Fat* 15.5g
- *Saturates* 1g

serves 4

Mixed Vegetable Curry with Chickpea Pancakes

Ingredients

200 g/7 oz carrots, cut into chunks

300 g/10¹/₂ oz potatoes, quartered

2 tbsp vegetable oil

1¹/₂ tsp cumin seeds

seeds from 5 green cardamom pods

1¹/₂ tsp mustard seeds

2 onions, grated

1 tsp ground turmeric

1 tsp ground coriander

1 bay leaf

1¹/₂ tsp chilli powder

1 tbsp grated fresh root ginger

2 large garlic cloves, crushed

250 ml/9 fl oz passata

200 ml/7 fl oz vegetable stock

115 g/4 oz frozen peas

115 g/4 oz frozen spinach leaves

salt

For the chickpea pancakes

225 g/8 oz gram or chickpea flour

1 tsp salt

¹/₂ tsp bicarbonate of soda

400 ml/14 fl oz water

vegetable oil, for frying

1 To make the pancakes, sift the flour, salt and bicarbonate of soda into a large mixing bowl. Make a well in the centre and add the water. Using a balloon whisk, gradually mix the flour into the water until you have a smooth batter. Leave to stand for 15 minutes.

2 Heat enough oil to cover the base of a frying pan over a medium heat. To make small pancakes, pour a small quantity of batter into the pan, or, if you prefer to make larger pancakes, swirl the pan to spread the batter mixture. Cook one side for 3 minutes, then, using a palette knife, turn over and cook the other side until golden. Keep warm while you repeat with the remaining batter to make 8 pancakes.

3 Meanwhile, to make the curry, put the carrots and potatoes into a steamer and steam until just tender but retaining some bite.

4 Heat the oil in a large, heavy-based saucepan over a medium heat and add the cumin seeds, cardamom seeds and mustard seeds. When they begin to darken and sizzle, add the onions, partially cover and cook over a medium-low heat, stirring frequently, for 10 minutes, or until soft and golden.

5 Add the other spices, ginger and garlic and cook, stirring constantly, for 1 minute. Add the passata, stock, potatoes and carrots, partially cover and cook for 10–15 minutes, or until the vegetables are tender. Add the peas and spinach, then cook for a further 2–3 minutes. Season to taste with salt before serving with the warm pancakes.

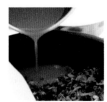

Nutritional Fact
Peas are a legume and therefore contain good levels of protein and soluble fibre to help maintain and clean out the bowel.

Serving Analysis

- *Calories*   *467*
- *Protein*   *19g*
- *Carbohydrate*   *72g*
- *Sugars*   *5.9g*
- *Fat*   *14g*
- *Saturates*   *1.4g*

serves 4

Spanish Tortilla

Ingredients

350 g/12 oz potatoes, cut into bite-sized cubes
1 tbsp olive oil
15 g/½ oz dairy-free margarine
1 onion, thinly sliced
6 eggs, lightly beaten
salt and pepper

1 Cook the potatoes in a saucepan of salted boiling water for 10–12 minutes, or until tender. Drain well and set aside.

2 Meanwhile, heat the oil and margarine in a medium-sized frying pan with a heatproof handle over a medium heat. Add the onion and fry, stirring occasionally, for 8 minutes, or until soft and golden. Add the potatoes and cook for a further 5 minutes, stirring to prevent them sticking. Spread the onions and potatoes evenly over the base of the pan.

3 Preheat the grill to medium. Season the eggs to taste with salt and pepper and pour over the onion and potatoes. Cook over a medium heat for 5–6 minutes, or until the eggs are just set and the base of the tortilla is lightly golden.

4 Place the pan under the preheated grill (if the handle is not heatproof, wrap with a double layer of foil) and cook the top of the tortilla for 2–3 minutes until it is just set and risen. Cut into wedges to serve.

Nutritional Fact
Potatoes are a good source of potassium, a highly beneficial mineral that helps the brain and nervous system to function.

Serving Analysis
- *Calories* 254
- *Protein* 11g
- *Carbohydrate* 21g
- *Sugars* 3g
- *Fat* 143g
- *Saturates* 2.8g

serves 4

Creamy Spinach & Mushroom Pasta

Ingredients

300 g/10¹/₂ oz dried gluten-free penne or pasta shape of your choice

salt and pepper

2 tbsp olive oil

250 g/9 oz mushrooms, sliced

1 tsp dried oregano

250 ml/9 fl oz vegetable stock

1 tbsp lemon juice

6 tbsp vegan cream cheese

200 g/7 oz frozen spinach leaves

Nutritional Fact

Spinach is high in potassium and folic acid and can help to reduce heart disease, eye degeneration and the risk of cancer.

Serving Analysis
- *Calories* 429
- *Protein* 13g
- *Carbohydrate* 61g
- *Sugars* 2.2g
- *Fat* 15g
- *Saturates* 2.3g

1 Cook the pasta in a large saucepan of lightly salted boiling water according to the packet instructions. Drain, reserving 175 ml/6 fl oz of the cooking liquid.

2 Meanwhile, heat the oil in a large, heavy-based frying pan over a medium heat, add the mushrooms and cook, stirring frequently, for 8 minutes, or until almost crisp. Stir in the oregano, stock and lemon juice and cook for 10–12 minutes, or until the sauce is reduced by half.

3 Stir in the cream cheese and spinach and cook over a medium-low heat for 3–5 minutes. Add the reserved cooking liquid, then the cooked pasta. Stir well, season to taste with salt and pepper and heat through before serving.

Nutritional Fact

Aubergines are a good source of folic acid, potassium and soluble fibre, which all help to clean and heal body tissues.

Serving Analysis

- *Calories*   488
- *Protein*   14g
- *Carbohydrate*   80g
- *Sugars*   16.8g
- *Fat*   14g
- *Saturates*   0.24g

serves 4

Aubergine Tagine with Polenta

1 Preheat the grill to medium. Toss the aubergine in 1 tablespoon of the oil and arrange in the grill pan. Cook under the preheated grill for 20 minutes, turning occasionally, until softened and beginning to blacken around the edges – brush with more oil if the aubergine becomes too dry.

2 Heat the remaining oil in a large, heavy-based saucepan over a medium heat. Add the onion and fry, stirring occasionally, for 8 minutes, or until soft and golden. Add the carrot, garlic and mushrooms and cook for 5 minutes. Add the spices and cook, stirring constantly, for a further minute.

3 Add the tomatoes and stock, stir well, then add the tomato purée. Bring to the boil, then reduce the heat and simmer for 10 minutes, or until the sauce begins to thicken and reduce.

4 Add the aubergine, apricots and chickpeas, partially cover and cook for a further 10 minutes, stirring occasionally.

5 Meanwhile, to make the polenta, pour the hot stock into a non-stick saucepan and bring to the boil. Pour in the polenta in a steady stream, stirring constantly with a wooden spoon. Reduce the heat to low and cook for 1–2 minutes, or until the polenta thickens to a mashed potato-like consistency. Serve the tagine with the polenta, sprinkled with the fresh coriander.

Ingredients

1 aubergine, cut into 1-cm/^{1}/$_2$-inch cubes

3 tbsp olive oil

1 large onion, thinly sliced

1 carrot, diced

2 garlic cloves, chopped

115 g/4 oz brown-cap mushrooms, sliced

2 tsp ground coriander

2 tsp cumin seeds

1 tsp chilli powder

1 tsp ground turmeric

600 ml/1 pint canned chopped tomatoes

300 ml/10 fl oz vegetable stock

1 tbsp tomato purée

75 g/2^3/$_4$ oz no-soak dried apricots, roughly chopped

400 g/14 oz canned chickpeas, drained and rinsed

2 tbsp fresh coriander, to garnish

For the polenta

1.2 litres/2 pints hot vegetable stock

200 g/7 oz instant polenta

salt and pepper

makes 8

Thai Tofu Cakes with Chilli Dip

Ingredients

300 g/10¹/₂ oz firm tofu (drained weight), coarsely grated

1 lemon grass stalk, outer layer discarded, finely chopped

2 garlic cloves, chopped

2.5-cm/1-inch piece fresh root ginger, grated

2 kaffir lime leaves, finely chopped (optional)

2 shallots, finely chopped

2 fresh red chillies, deseeded and finely chopped

4 tbsp chopped fresh coriander

90 g/3¹/₄ oz gluten-free plain flour, plus extra for flouring

¹/₂ tsp salt

sunflower oil, for frying

For the chilli dip

3 tbsp white distilled vinegar or rice wine vinegar

2 spring onions, finely sliced

1 tbsp caster sugar

2 fresh chillies, finely chopped

2 tbsp chopped fresh coriander

pinch of salt

Nutritional Fact

Tofu is a good source of protein that also contains B vitamins for energy and brain function and magnesium for calming the gut.

Serving Analysis

- Calories   130
- Protein   7.3g
- Carbohydrate   16g
- Sugars   4.3g
- Fat   4.9g
- Saturates   0.7g

1 To make the chilli dip, mix all the ingredients together in a small serving bowl and set aside.

2 Mix the tofu with the lemon grass, garlic, ginger, lime leaves, if using, shallots, chillies and coriander in a mixing bowl. Stir in the flour and salt to make a coarse, sticky paste. Cover and chill in the refrigerator for 1 hour to allow the mixture to firm up slightly.

3 Form the mixture into large walnut-sized balls and, using floured hands, flatten into rounds until you have 8 cakes. Heat enough oil to cover the base of a large, heavy-based frying pan over a medium heat. Cook the cakes in 2 batches, turning halfway through, for 4–6 minutes, or until golden brown. Drain on kitchen paper and serve warm with the chilli dip.

serves 4

Roasted Butternut Squash Risotto

1 Preheat the oven to 200°C/400°F/Gas Mark 6. Put the squash into a roasting tin. Mix 1 tablespoon of the oil with the honey and spoon over the squash. Turn the squash to coat it in the mixture. Roast in the preheated oven for 30–35 minutes, or until tender.

2 Meanwhile, put the basil and oregano into a food processor with 2 tablespoons of the remaining oil and process until finely chopped and blended. Set aside.

3 Heat the margarine and remaining oil in a large, heavy-based saucepan over a medium heat. Add the onions and fry, stirring occasionally, for 8 minutes, or until soft and golden. Add the rice and cook for 2 minutes, stirring to coat the grains in the oil mixture.

4 Pour in the wine and bring to the boil. Reduce the heat slightly and cook until the wine is almost absorbed. Add the stock, a little at a time, and cook over a medium-low heat, stirring constantly, for 20 minutes.

5 Gently stir in the herb oil and squash until thoroughly mixed into the rice and cook for a further 5 minutes, or until the rice is creamy and cooked but retaining a little bite in the centre of the grain. Season well with salt and pepper before serving.

Nutritional Fact

Butternut squash and pumpkin are high in the antioxidant betacarotene, which protects against damage from UV light.

Serving Analysis

• Calories	436
• Protein	5.8g
• Carbohydrate	59g
• Sugars	9.3g
• Fat	17.5g
• Saturates	0.6g

Ingredients

600 g/1 lb 5 oz butternut squash or pumpkin, peeled and cut into bite-sized pieces

4 tbsp olive oil

1 tsp clear honey

25 g/1 oz fresh basil

25 g/1 oz fresh oregano

1 tbsp dairy-free margarine

2 onions, finely chopped

450 g/1 lb arborio or other risotto rice

175 ml/6 fl oz dry white wine

1.2 litres/2 pints vegetable stock

salt and pepper

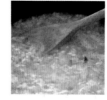

Desserts & Baking

Delicious delights await you in this chapter. Sweet treats include rich, fudgy chocolate brownies, a sticky orange and almond cake and a creamy mango baked cheesecake. Friends and family will be amazed that they are entirely wheat-, gluten- and dairy-free. If you are looking for a healthy end to a meal, there's the refreshing pear and ginger granita.

serves 4–6

Pear & Ginger Granita

Ingredients

75 g/2³/₄ oz caster sugar

1 tbsp clear honey

250 ml/9 fl oz water

225 g/8 oz just-ripe pears, peeled, cored and sliced

2 tsp finely chopped fresh root ginger

3 tbsp lemon juice

1 Put the sugar, honey and water into a saucepan over a medium heat and heat, stirring, until the sugar has dissolved. Add the pears and ginger and simmer for 5 minutes, then add the lemon juice.

2 Tip the pears and cooking liquid into a food processor or blender and process until almost smooth. Carefully pour the mixture into a freezerproof container with a lid and leave to cool.

3 Put in the freezer for 2 hours until the edges and bottom of the pear mixture are frozen. Remove the container from the freezer and mix with a fork so that the frozen part of the mixture is blended with the unfrozen part. Replace the lid and return to the freezer for a further 1¹/₂ hours.

4 Repeat the mixing process and freeze for a further hour until the mixture forms ice crystals. Serve at this stage or return to the freezer until required, then remove 30 minutes before serving and mix again with a fork. Serve spooned into glasses.

Nutritional Fact
Like apples, pears contain high levels of pectin, a type of fibre that is particularly good at carrying toxins out of the body and reducing blood cholesterol.

Serving Analysis

- Calories   100
- Protein   0.2g
- Carbohydrate   26g
- Sugars   22g
- Fat   0.2g
- Saturates   0.01g

serves 4

Apple & Plum Crumble

1 Preheat the oven to 180°C/350°F/Gas Mark 4. Mix the apples, plums, apple juice and sugar together in a 23-cm/9-inch round pie dish.

2 To make the topping, sift the flour into a mixing bowl and rub in the margarine with your fingertips until it resembles coarse breadcrumbs. Stir in the buckwheat and rice flakes, sunflower seeds, sugar and cinnamon, then spoon the topping over the fruit in the dish.

3 Bake the crumble in the preheated oven for 30–35 minutes, or until the topping is lightly browned and crisp.

Ingredients

4 apples, peeled, cored and diced

5 plums, halved, stoned and quartered

4 tbsp fresh apple juice

25 g/1 oz soft light brown sugar

For the topping

115 g/4 oz gluten-free flour

75 g/2³/₄ oz dairy-free margarine, diced

25 g/1 oz buckwheat flakes

25 g/1 oz rice flakes

25 g/1 oz sunflower seeds

50 g/1³/₄ oz soft light brown sugar

¹/₄ tsp ground cinnamon

Nutritional Fact
Apples and plums both release their sugars slowly and do not cause a sudden, undesirable rush of sugar into the bloodstream.

Serving Analysis
- *Calories*   495
- *Protein*   18g
- *Carbohydrate*   71g
- *Sugars*   43.5g
- *Fat*   19.5g
- *Saturates*   2.5g

serves 8

Chocolate Orange Mousse Cake

 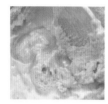 

Ingredients

100 g/3¹/₂ oz caster sugar

100 g/3¹/₂ oz dairy-free margarine, plus extra for greasing

2 eggs, lightly beaten

100 g/3¹/₂ oz gluten-free plain flour

1 tsp gluten-free baking powder

2 tbsp cocoa powder

finely pared strips of orange rind, to decorate

For the mousse

200 g/7 oz good-quality plain dark chocolate (about 70 per cent cocoa solids)

grated rind of 2 oranges and juice of 1

4 eggs, separated

1 Preheat the oven to 180°C/350°F/Gas Mark 4. Grease a 23-cm/9-inch round, loose-bottomed cake tin and line the base.

2 Cream the sugar and margarine together in a mixing bowl until pale and fluffy. Gradually add the eggs, beating well with a wooden spoon between each addition. Sift the flour, baking powder and cocoa powder together, fold half into the egg mixture, then fold in the remainder. Spoon the mixture into the prepared tin and level the surface with the back of a spoon. Bake in the preheated oven for 20 minutes until risen and firm to the touch. Leave in the tin to cool completely.

3 Meanwhile, melt the chocolate in a heatproof bowl placed over a saucepan of gently simmering water, making sure that the bottom of the bowl does not touch the water. Leave to cool, then stir in the orange rind and juice and the egg yolks.

4 Whisk the egg whites in a large bowl until they form stiff peaks. Gently fold a large spoonful of the egg whites into the chocolate mixture, then fold in the remainder. Spoon the mixture on top of the cooked, cooled sponge and level the top with the back of a spoon. Alternatively, remove the sponge from the tin, slice through and sandwich with the mousse. Place in the refrigerator to set. Remove the sides of the tin if not removed earlier (though not the base) before decorating with the strips of orange rind and serving.

Nutritional Fact

Chocolate contains catechins, which are antioxidant plant chemicals, similar to those found in fruits and vegetables.

Serving Analysis

• Calories	370
• Protein	7g
• Carbohydrate	38.5g
• Sugars	25g
• Fat	22.8g
• Saturates	8.4g

makes 12 brownies

Super Mocha Brownies

Ingredients

150 g/5¹/₂ oz good-quality plain dark chocolate (about 70 per cent cocoa solids)

100 g/3¹/₂ oz dairy-free margarine, plus extra for greasing

1 tsp strong instant coffee

1 tsp vanilla extract

100 g/3¹/₂ oz ground almonds

175 g/6 oz caster sugar

4 eggs, separated

icing sugar, to decorate (optional)

  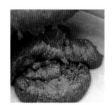

Nutritional Fact

Dark chocolate contains more cocoa solids than milk chocolate, and has, therefore, more beneficial properties.

Serving Analysis

• *Calories*	*254*
• *Protein*	*4.5g*
• *Carbohydrate*	*24g*
• *Sugars*	*20.5g*
• *Fat*	*17g*
• *Saturates*	*4.7g*

1 Preheat the oven to 180°C/350°F/Gas Mark 4. Grease a 20-cm/8-inch square cake tin and line the base.

2 Melt the chocolate and margarine in a heatproof bowl placed over a saucepan of gently simmering water, making sure that the bottom of the bowl does not touch the water. Stir very occasionally until the chocolate and margarine have melted and are smooth.

3 Carefully remove the bowl from the heat. Leave to cool slightly, then stir in the coffee and vanilla extract. Add the almonds and sugar and mix well until combined. Lightly beat the egg yolks in a separate bowl, then stir into the chocolate mixture.

4 Whisk the egg whites in a large bowl until they form stiff peaks. Gently fold a large spoonful of the egg whites into the chocolate mixture, then fold in the remainder until completely incorporated.

5 Spoon the mixture into the prepared tin and bake in the preheated oven for 35–40 minutes, or until risen and firm on top but still slightly gooey in the centre. Leave to cool in the tin, then turn out, remove the lining paper and cut into 12 pieces. Dust with icing sugar before serving, if liked.

serves 8

Mango & Maple Cheesecake

Ingredients

70 g/2¹/₂ oz dairy-free margarine, plus extra for greasing

175 g/6 oz gluten- and dairy-free biscuits, such as digestives, crushed

40 g/1¹/₂ oz ground almonds

For the filling

1 large mango, stoned, peeled and diced

juice of 1 lemon

200 g/7 oz natural soya yogurt

1 tbsp gluten-free cornflour

3 tbsp maple syrup

450 g/1 lb vegan cream cheese

For the topping

3 tbsp maple syrup

1 small mango, stoned, peeled and sliced

1 Preheat the oven to 180°C/350°F/Gas Mark 4. Lightly grease a 23-cm/9-inch round, loose-bottomed cake tin. To make the biscuit base, melt the margarine in a medium-sized saucepan, then stir in the crushed biscuits and almonds. Then press the mixture into the base of the prepared cake tin to make an even layer. Bake in the preheated oven for 10 minutes.

2 Meanwhile, to make the filling, put the mango, lemon juice, yogurt, cornflour, maple syrup and cream cheese into a food processor or blender and process until smooth and creamy. Pour the mixture over the biscuit base and smooth with the back of a spoon. Bake for 25–30 minutes, or until golden and set. Leave to cool in the tin, then transfer to a wire rack and chill in the refrigerator for 30 minutes to firm up.

3 To make the topping, heat the maple syrup in a frying pan. Brush the top of the cheesecake with the maple syrup. Add the mango to the remaining maple syrup in the pan and cook for 1 minute, stirring. Leave to cool slightly, then arrange the mango slices on top of the cheesecake. Pour over any remaining syrup before serving.

Nutritional Fact
Mangoes are a rich source of beta-carotene and other carotenoids, the plant chemicals that provide their rich golden colour and help to protect the body.

Serving Analysis

• Calories	464
• Protein	8g
• Carbohydrate	35g
• Sugars	22g
• Fat	34.5g
• Saturates	4g

makes 9 slices

Orange & Almond Syrup Cake

Ingredients

dairy-free margarine, for greasing

6 eggs, separated

200 g/7 oz caster sugar

grated rind of 3 oranges

150 g/5¹/₂ oz ground almonds

For the topping

juice of 3 oranges

3 tbsp clear honey

Nutritional Fact
Almonds help to balance blood sugar and so when they are used in a sweet dish, they help to dilute the effects of a sudden rush of sugar.

Serving Analysis
• *Calories*	*269*
• *Protein*	*7.9g*
• *Carbohydrate*	*34g*
• *Sugars*	*30g*
• *Fat*	*12.3g*
• *Saturates*	*1.8g*

1 Preheat the oven to 180°C/350°F/Gas Mark 4. Grease a 20-cm/8-inch square cake tin and line the base. Beat the egg yolks with the sugar, orange rind and almonds in a large mixing bowl.

2 Whisk the egg whites in a separate large bowl until they form stiff peaks. Fold a spoonful of the egg whites into the almond mixture, then fold in the remainder. Carefully pour the mixture into the prepared cake tin.

3 Bake in the preheated oven for 45–50 minutes, or until a skewer inserted into the centre of the cake comes out clean. Leave to cool in the tin.

4 To make the topping, put the orange juice and honey into a small saucepan and bring to the boil, stir once, then cook, without stirring, for 6–8 minutes, or until reduced, thickened and syrupy. Using a fork, pierce the cake all over, then pour the syrup over the top and leave to soak in before serving.

makes 12

Banana Muffins with Cinnamon Frosting

Ingredients

150 g/5^1/$_2$ oz gluten-free plain flour

1 tsp gluten-free baking powder

pinch of salt

150 g/5^1/$_2$ oz caster sugar

6 tbsp dairy-free milk

2 eggs, lightly beaten

150 g/5^1/$_2$ oz dairy-free margarine, melted

2 small bananas, mashed

For the frosting

50 g/1^3/$_4$ oz vegan cream cheese

2 tbsp dairy-free margarine

^{1}/$_4$ tsp ground cinnamon

90 g/3^1/$_4$ oz icing sugar

Nutritional Fact

Cinnamon, like almonds, helps to balance blood sugar and reduce the ill-effects of sweet foods.

Serving Analysis

• Calories	272
• Protein	2.7g
• Carbohydrate	34g
• Sugars	22g
• Fat	14.5g
• Saturates	2.8g

1 Preheat the oven to 200°C/400°F/Gas Mark 6. Place 12 large paper cases in a deep muffin tin. Sift the flour, baking powder and salt together into a mixing bowl. Stir in the sugar.

2 Whisk the milk, eggs and margarine together in a separate bowl until combined. Slowly stir into the flour mixture without beating. Fold in the mashed bananas.

3 Spoon the mixture into the paper cases and bake in the preheated oven for 20 minutes until risen and golden. Turn out on to a wire rack and leave to cool.

4 To make the frosting, beat the cream cheese and margarine together in a bowl, then beat in the cinnamon and icing sugar until smooth and creamy. Chill the frosting in the refrigerator for about 15 minutes to firm up, then top each muffin with a spoonful.

makes one 450 g/1 lb loaf

Red Pepper Cornbread

Nutritional Fact

Red peppers contain the chemical capsaicin, which is thought to soothe the pain of indigestion.

Serving Analysis

- Calories   104
- Protein   5.9g
- Carbohydrate   12.2g
- Sugars   0.9g
- Fat   4g
- Saturates   0.3g

Ingredients

1 large red pepper, deseeded and sliced
175 g/6 oz fine cornmeal or polenta
115 g/4 oz gluten-free strong white flour
1 tbsp gluten-free baking powder
1 tsp salt
2 tsp sugar
250 ml/9 fl oz dairy-free milk
2 eggs, lightly beaten
3 tbsp olive oil, plus extra for oiling

1 Preheat the oven to 200°C/400°F/Gas Mark 6. Lightly oil a 450 g/1 lb loaf tin. Arrange the red pepper slices on a baking tray and roast in the preheated oven for 35 minutes until tender and the skin begins to blister. Set aside to cool slightly, then peel away the skin.

2 Meanwhile, mix the cornmeal, flour, baking powder, salt and sugar together in a large mixing bowl. Beat the milk, eggs and oil together in a separate bowl or jug and gradually add to the flour mixture. Beat with a wooden spoon to make a thick, smooth, batter-like consistency.

3 Finely chop the red pepper and fold into the cornmeal mixture, then spoon into the prepared tin. Bake in the preheated oven for 30 minutes until lightly golden. Leave in the tin for 10 minutes, then run a knife around the edge of the tin and turn the loaf out on to a wire rack to cool. To keep fresh, wrap the loaf in foil or seal in a polythene bag.

Index